MW00760026

HOPE

PEACE

LOVE

JOY

HOPE

PEACE

LOVE

JOY

MARCIA HOTCHKISS
& GILDA HURST

Cover & Text Design: Sarah Mock Griffin
Spanish Translation: Dee Anna Villalobos

Paperback ISBN: 978-1-942243-41-0
E-book ISBN: 978-1-942243-42-7
Library of Congress Control Number: 2020920504

CONTENTS

FOREWORD

ADVENT 2020

OUR SOCIETY often expects Christmas to look like a Norman Rockwell painting. However, very few of us live up to that ideal. Advent, or the weeks leading up to Christmas, can be a challenge. Pressure is everywhere. Buying gifts, cooking meals, and interacting with family and friends can all be draining. Sometimes we wonder if it's worth it.

The season of Advent helps Christians focus on what is really important. We expect a baby who will bring the world glad tidings of great joy (Luke 2:10). The God of the universe loves each of us so much that he became a helpless infant and lived and died for us. Just when we needed a Savior, God sent one.

Our prayer with these daily devotions is to connect you with the love that came to reach us. May the light of Advent shine so we will know the one for whom we are waiting and the blessings he brings.

HOPE

First Sunday of Advent

Almighty God, give us grace to cast away the works of darkness, and put on the armor of light, now in the time of this mortal life in which your Son Jesus Christ came to visit us in great humility; that in the last day, when he shall come again in his glorious majesty to judge both the living and the dead, we may rise to the life immortal; through him who lives and reigns with you and the Holy Spirit, one God, now and for ever. *Amen.*

Book of Common Prayer, Collect for the First Sunday of Advent

Sunday, November 29

Read Isaiah 64:1-9.

"Yet, O LORD, you are our Father; we are the clay, and you are our potter; we are all the work of your hand." — Isaiah 64:8

THIS VERSE FROM ISAIAH is from a bigger reading that explains in detail how all of us have failed to live up to God's perfection. We humans play a dangerous guessing game called, "Who will live with God forever?" by comparing ourselves favorably with other people. But the Bible clearly says that we have to be perfect, and as mere mortals, we always miss the mark.

So, what should we take from this on the first Sunday of Advent 2020? First, we are children of God. The Lord made us with his own hand. That makes us more precious than anything else, and it signals to all that we are loved beyond measure.

Also, as we begin this Advent season, it reminds us that God loved us so much that he couldn't leave us to the fate we deserve. Instead, the Lord sent his only begotten Son into the world so that we would be reconciled to him.

Lord, help me grasp the knowledge that you love me completely and you come to save us.

MONDAY, NOVEMBER 30

Read Isaiah 1:10-20.

"Trample my courts no more; bringing offerings is futile; incense is an abomination to me. New moon and sabbath and calling of convocation—I cannot endure solemn assemblies with iniquity. Your new moons and your appointed festivals my soul hates; they have become a burden to me, I am weary of bearing them." — Isaiah 1:12b-14

IN THIS READING, the Lord is proclaiming that He does not value outward appearances but rather the condition of our hearts. He even goes so far as to say these surface offerings make him weary.

How often do we think of God as weary? Probably not very often. I have Amy Grant's album *Be Still and Know* downloaded on my phone. My favorite song is "Carry You" with the words, "I'm weary watching while you struggle on your own. Call my name, I'll come." This means that I don't have to construct plans and ways to get to God on my own. He comes, as we are told in Advent, most clearly when I confess my efforts are futile.

Lord, help me know in my heart and head that nothing I can do or say can make you love me any more or less. You come because of who you are, and only you can carry me.

Tuesday, December 1

Read John 1:35-42.

"The next day John again was standing with two of his disciples, and as he watched Jesus walk by, he exclaimed, 'Look, here is the Lamb of God!' The two disciples heard him say this, and they followed Jesus. When Jesus turned and saw them following, he said to them, 'What are you looking for?' They said to him, 'Rabbi' (which translated means Teacher), 'where are you staying?' He said to them, 'Come and see.'"
— John 1:35-39a

THIS READING FROM JOHN always amazes me for its evangelical simplicity. After John recognized Jesus as the Messiah, the two disciples left behind whatever they were doing and followed Jesus. When the men asked Jesus where he is staying, he simply told them to "come and see."

We see Philip also telling Nathaniel to, "Come and see," a few verses later in this first chapter of John. Another simple statement that does not push or manipulate; rather, it simply invites.

I see this same inviting nature of God gently nudging me. I have heard it said that God does not force himself upon us because he is gentle and polite. I think it is also because he knows my rebellious nature. He knows that I run whenever I feel cornered. The Lord tells me to "come and see" because it is much more likely I will eventually respond to him.

Lord, help me follow when you say, "Come and see."

Wednesday, December 2

Read 1 Thessalonians 2:13-20.

"We also constantly give thanks to God for this, that when you received the word of God that you heard from us, you accepted it not as a human word but as what it really is, God's word, which is also at work in you believers. For you, brothers and sisters, became imitators of the churches of God in Christ Jesus that are in Judea, for you suffered the same things from your own compatriots as they did from the Jews." — 1 Thessalonians 2:13-14

THE APOSTLE PAUL here writes about the faithfulness of the believers at Thessalonica. He says that they accepted the word of God for exactly what it is, and they are imitators of the Christians in Judea. In other words, not only have the Thessalonians been converted but they are also being transformed by their faith. Secretly, I often do not want to be transformed because I am afraid that God will change something important to me like my relationships, my time, or my money.

What form does resistance to the Holy Spirit take in your life? We usually want to hang on to control and direction, and we often do so even when the results are not what we really want. The first step in any 12-step program is to say that I am powerless (over drugs, alcohol, other people, etc.). That is also the beginning of being transformed by

the living God. When we admit we need God, then we let
down the walls and resistances that we have built up, and
that is the first step to being truly transformed.

Lord, help me to be open to transformation by the Holy Spirit.

Thursday, December 3

Read 1 Thessalonians 3:1-13.

"Therefore when we could bear it no longer, we decided to be left alone in Athens; and we sent Timothy, our brother and co-worker for God in proclaiming the gospel of Christ, to strengthen and encourage you for the sake of your faith, so that no one would be shaken by these persecutions. Indeed, you yourselves know that this is what we are destined for. In fact, when we were with you, we told you beforehand that we were to suffer persecution; so it turned out, as you know. For this reason, when I could bear it no longer, I sent to find out about your faith; I was afraid that somehow the tempter had tempted you and that our labour had been in vain."

— *1 Thessalonians 3:1-5*

WE OFTEN THINK of Paul as a force of nature, but in this reading from his first letter to the Thessalonians, we see the importance of human relationships to him. On one hand, Paul seems to be coolly stating the inevitability of being persecuted. On the other hand, he seems to be acknowledging a deep love and concern for these brothers and sisters in Christ. In fact, he even says more than once that he "could bear it no longer" when he did not get a report on them and their faith.

I heard a speaker at a women's conference once ask the attendees to project to the end of our lives and consider what would be important then. Of course, God and his Word would loom quite large, but what else? The people we had loved and the people who loved us.

God, please help me to remember that the people in my life are created and redeemed by you and are more important than deadlines or disagreements or agendas or politics. And those relationships may very well reflect my true religion, what I really believe about you.

Friday, December 4

Read Luke 20:41-21:4.

"He looked up and saw rich people putting their gifts into the treasury; he also saw a poor widow put in two small copper coins. He said, 'Truly I tell you, this poor widow has put in more than all of them; for all of them have contributed out of their abundance, but she out of her poverty has put in all she had to live on.'" — Luke 21:1-4

JESUS CALLS OUT the rich people giving their excess money in the synagogue and commends the poor widow who merely puts in two coins. The Bible certainly mentions money a lot, but I wonder if there is a deeper message. First, in the Judea of Jesus' time and every other time since then, we humans often hold our money and how we spend it in a hidden but clenched fist. Maybe this is because too often our worth as people is measured by the money or possessions we have. As Ignatius of Loyola taught, disciples should hold all worldly things, including money, lightly. Money is a gift of God, and it need not be too tightly grasped.

Secondly, maybe this Gospel story also talks about our bigger resistance to God. We often resist the work of the Holy Spirit in our lives when something too important to us is in play. We want to only give God the parts of our lives that we choose and that won't change our worlds.

But the poor (in fact and in spirit) know all too well their desperate need for God and fling their entire lives at his feet.

Jesus, remind me often of my desperate and sometimes hidden need for you.

Saturday, December 5

Read 1 Thessalonians 4:13-18.

"But we do not want you to be uninformed, brothers and sisters, about those who have died, so that you may not grieve as others do who have no hope. For since we believe that Jesus died and rose again, even so, through Jesus, God will bring with him those who have died. For this we declare to you by the word of the Lord, that we who are alive, who are left until the coming of the Lord, will by no means precede those who have died. For the Lord himself, with a cry of command, with the archangel's call and with the sound of God's trumpet, will descend from heaven, and the dead in Christ will rise first. Then we who are alive, who are left, will be caught up in the clouds together with them to meet the Lord in the air; and so we will be with the Lord forever. Therefore encourage one another with these words."— 1 Thessalonians 4:13-18

THIS READING of Paul's letter to the Thessalonians highlights the importance of knowing the truth about our eternal home. For most of us, this is reassuring. Although God wants us to be fully engaged and present with what is going on around us, the truth is that this world is not our ultimate destination.

Amy Simpson in *Blessed Are the Unsatisfied* says that our goal should never be to find total contentment here. "As we look toward a better world, we exercise our faith in what we cannot see (Hebrews 11:1). And what is visible to us now, we see a hazy reflection in a mirror, knowing that someday we will see face to face, and our knowledge, incomplete and unsatisfied for now, will then be complete (1 Corinthians 13:9-12)."

I praise God that one day we will be with the Lord and no longer struggle with issues of appearance, broken relationships, injustice, and hatred.

God, help me to see your grace at work in this world and know that it is a foretaste of the glorious and heavenly home to come.

PEACE

SECOND SUNDAY OF ADVENT

Merciful God, who sent your messengers the prophets to preach repentance and prepare the way for our salvation: Give us grace to heed their warnings and forsake our sins, that we may greet with joy the coming of Jesus Christ our Redeemer; who lives and reigns with you and the Holy Spirit, one God, now and for ever. *Amen.*

Book of Common Prayer, Collect for the Second Sunday of Advent

Sunday, December 6

Read Mark 1:1-8.
"I have baptized you with water; but he will baptize you with the Holy Spirit."— Mark 1:8

GOD CALLED John the Baptist to prepare the people of Israel for the coming of the Messiah who is to live among us and within us. His call is for us to open our hearts, to turn from the poison of sin, and to receive Jesus. That same call to preparedness echoes loudly today.

What message of hope and preparation does Jesus promise for us who are experiencing exile due to a pandemic, or racial division, or both? How do we begin to unravel the fear, hatred, violence, isolation, anger, depression, disobedience, and downward spiraling desires to grab hold of the eternal hope found in the *water* of baptism? It is the *water* that released us once and for all from the death of sin. It is *eternal water* that cleanses not only the external but also remakes us internally: an authentic creation, made ready for the Holy Spirit that resides and actively guides us.

Carrie Underwood's song "Something in the Water" seems to magnify the change and strength that occurs in the water: "Got joy in my heart, angels on my side. Thank God almighty, I saw the light. There must be something in the water."

Lord, prepare my body, mind, and spirit for this time and season to willingly enter the water of fulfillment.

Monday, December 7

Read 1 Thessalonians 5:1-11.

"But you, beloved, are not in darkness, for that day to surprise you like a thief; for you are all children of the light and children of the day; we are not of the night or of darkness."— 1 Thessalonians 5:4-5

AS CERTAIN AS the sun rising and the moon shining in the darkness, the Messiah is coming. I love that St. Paul identifies us as children of the light and children of the day. Advent is full of images of light and darkness. Automobile headlights, streetlights, lighthouses, and security lights all illuminate space to navigate us to safety. My favorite lighting is on a string. Whether it is wrapped around a tree or suspended across open spaces, there is something exciting, creating positive anticipation.

Life lures us to hide in the darkness. And the darkness, with its promise of secrecy in activities that destroy, creates chaos and wreaks havoc. St. Paul warns us to be alert and to have self-control for we "know not the hour" when Christ will return.

The Messiah is coming. *"Let us be sober, and put on the breastplate of faith and love, and for a helmet the hope of salvation. For God has destined us not for wrath but for obtaining salvation through our Lord Jesus Christ"*

(1 Thess. 5:8b-9). We are children of the light and children of the day.

Lord, as the lights shine around us this Advent, let our hearts also examine the darkness within and welcome the light which illuminates.

Tuesday, December 8

Read 1 Thessalonians 5:12-28.

"Be at peace among yourselves. And we urge you, beloved, to admonish the idlers, encourage the faint-hearted, help the weak, be patient with all of them. See that none of you repays evil for evil, but always seek to do good to one another and to all."— 1 Thessalonians 5:13b-15

OUR CHILDHOOD SUMMERS were spent building forts in the hay barn and exploring the woods with my brother. Cutting across the field and through the garden heading home, my brother's mischief could not resist the vine ripened tomatoes that quickly became his ammunition. I was the target! The shrieks of insults and nonsense ensued, and it was all-out war. Just as suddenly as it started, a cease-fire was commanded: "Dewain! Gilda! Stop right now!" Mom was on the scene. "He started it!" I replied. "She was throwing tomatoes, too!" Dewain defended. My mom's voice echoes even now as I heard her say, *"Do to others as you would have them do to you"* (Luke 6:31).

In this reading, Paul points us back to the Golden Rule of treating each other with respect, love, and patience, and treating even those who have wronged us with kindness. It takes prayer and practice for our thoughts to come in alignment with our hearts—and for our actions to align with both.

Advent brings a gathering time for family and friends. Are there rotten tomato memories clutched in your fist, ready for fresh fights over past wounds? Christ's example of praying continually for God's will promises a heart filled with joy.

Holy Spirit, we open our hands for you to guide us to live in peace with each other.

WEDNESDAY, DECEMBER 9

Read Isaiah 6:1-13.

"And I said: 'Woe to me! I am lost, for I am a man of unclean lips, and I live among a people of unclean lips; yet my eyes have seen the King, the LORD of hosts!' Then one of the seraphs flew to me, holding a live coal that had been taken from the altar with a pair of tongs. The seraph touched my mouth with it and said: 'Now that this has touched your lips, your guilt has departed and your sin is blotted out."
— *Isaiah 6:5-7*

CAN YOU IMAGINE a hot, searing coal placed on your tender lips? Why might God have chosen the lips to sear? According to speech language experts, lips change the resonance of speech sounds. When compressed and then opened, they produce rapid, explosive release of breath. Breath. Pneuma. The coals sear the lips for the Spirit emerging from deep within our hearts.

Guilt is gone and sins blotted out. Release. What live coal needs to touch your lips? What will break the chains that shackle us to our sin?

Lord, choose the coal that purifies heart, mind, spirit, and soul that we may be worthy and answer God's call on our lives.

Thursday, December 10

Read Luke 22:1-13.

"'Make preparations for us there.' So they went and found everything as he had told them, and they prepared the Passover meal." — Luke 22:12b-13

DAY TWELVE OF ADVENT brings us to The Last Supper preparations. Peter and John were selected by Jesus to go before him to find the appointed upper room, buy the groceries, prepare the food according to Kosher laws, tidy the area, adorn the banquet table with prescribed table settings, prepare foot-washing basins, and all the other essential items. I wonder if they had a detailed checklist complete with a seating chart! If you have ever hosted a big event, you know the importance of details and a timetable. Yet, they were clueless that this Passover was about to be a covenant changer.

The Passover of old required an annual sacrifice of an unblemished lamb accompanied by specific side dishes, detailed preparation, cooking, eating requirements for the forgiveness of sins. Jesus was turning the tables to create a new covenant. Jesus, the perfect Lamb of God, would be sacrificed, sealing the forgiveness of sin forever.

A peace floods over me as I ponder Jesus' sacrifice. He simplified forgiveness so everyone could sit at the banquet table forgiven forever. What unforgiveness is clinging to your soul? Come and recline with Jesus and tell him your story. All are invited to the table.

Lord, give us eyes to see, ears to hear, and hearts to receive your Passover gift of taking away the sin of the world.

Friday, December 11

Read Isaiah 7:10-25.
"Again the LORD spoke to Ahaz, saying, 'Ask a sign of the LORD your God; let it be deep as Sheol or high as heaven.' But Ahaz said, 'I will not ask, and I will not put the LORD to the test.'" — Isaiah 7:10-12

GOD OFFERS A SIGN! Ahaz rejects God's grace and mercy for his own plan. He is warned of the impending destruction of his people and kingdom if he proceeds. And he does it anyway.

Comedian Bill Engvall has made a fortune making his audiences laugh with his "Here's Your Sign" routines. We laugh and shake our heads over the crazy things people say or do while not thinking it through before they act.

Signs can rest in the tension between negative and positive outcomes. Sometimes we ignore the lump in the breast for fear of what the sign indicates. When one acknowledges the sign and creates a health care team and a nutritional plan, it can provide a very different journey from doing nothing. However, when one ignores signs due to the fear of losing peers, social status, change in economic status, beliefs, traditions, and possible relocation, all can stifle us from God's sign of grace. Praying together in unity, asking for signs, and then actively seeking those signs can release an abundance of God's mercy. Either way, ignoring or seeking, we need to be ready to accept the consequences.

Lord, you sent the Holy Spirit to guide us, to comfort us. Open our eyes and hearts to the signs you provide for our lives.

Saturday, December 12

Read Luke 22:31-38.

"Simon, Simon, listen! Satan has demanded to sift all of you like wheat, but I have prayed for you that your own faith may not fail; and you, when once you have turned back, strengthen your brothers."— Luke 22:31-32

THE DEVIL is our adversary looking for someone to devour (1 Peter 5:8)—someone to distract, discourage, and confuse. Satan's desire for power sought to expose Peter and the disciples' weaknesses to break their faith. But there was Jesus illuminating the past tense of Satan's scheme to Peter. Jesus had *prayed* for the strength of Peter's faith, and he reassured Peter that he would turn back and strengthen others.

Zach Williams wrote the song "There Was Jesus" and recorded it with Dolly Parton. Zach shared his life story of being sifted by Satan. That sifting of his weakness is now heard by millions as a testimony of how we never walk alone:

> In the waiting, in the searching,
> In the healing, in the hurting
> Like a blessing buried in the broken pieces
> Every minute, every moment
> Where I've been or where I'm going

Even when I didn't know it
Or couldn't see it
There was Jesus

Jesus has a gift waiting for you this Advent. All the broken pieces the adversary meant for harm, Jesus restores into a beautiful testimony.

Jesus, reveal our broken-pieces story unmasking the enemy while disclosing your ever-present healing, grace, and mercy.

LOVE

THIRD SUNDAY OF ADVENT

Stir up your power, O Lord, and with great might come among us; and, because we are sorely hindered by our sins, let your bountiful grace and mercy speedily help and deliver us; through Jesus Christ our Lord, to whom, with you and the Holy Spirit, be honor and glory, now and for ever. *Amen.*

Book of Common Prayer, Collect for the Third Sunday of Advent

SUNDAY, DECEMBER 13

Read John 1:6-8, 19-28 .

"There was a man sent from God, whose name was John. He came as a witness to testify to the light, so that all might believe through him. He himself was not the light, but he came to testify to the light ."— John 1:6-8

IN THIS READING and others about John the Baptist, he appears to be humble but completely comfortable in his calling from God. John is not ego-driven like many in the world and in the church. We all can name ministries that were personality-driven, rather than Spirit-driven. Often the experience leaves us disappointed and discouraged.

On the other hand, John's role is one that we can imitate. The Word says that John *"himself was not the light, but he came to testify to the light."* In a similar and possibly a less dramatic way, we Christians can point to the true light that came into the world at Christmas. We can find the story of Jesus just as compelling as John did. I doubt many of us will suffer John's ultimate fate, but we can all show a suffering and fallen world the Light by pointing out God's grace in every place we see it.

Help us, Lord, to testify only to you.

Monday, December 14

Read Luke 22:39-53.

"He came out and went, as was his custom, to the Mount of Olives; and the disciples followed him. When he reached the place, he said to them, 'Pray that you may not come into the time of trial.' Then he withdrew from them about a stone's throw, knelt down, and prayed, 'Father, if you are willing, remove this cup from me; yet, not my will but yours be done.' Then an angel from heaven appeared to him and gave him strength. In his anguish he prayed more earnestly, and his sweat became like great drops of blood falling down on the ground. When he got up from prayer, he came to the disciples and found them sleeping because of grief, and he said to them, 'Why are you sleeping? Get up and pray that you may not come into the time of trial.'"— Luke 22:39-46

DURING THIS TIME OF YEAR, the focus is on the birth of the Savior. We, like Ricky Bobby (Will Ferrell) in the comedy "Talladega Nights," find comfort in thinking about "little 8 lb., 6 oz. cuddly baby Jesus." But this Gospel story from Luke helps us think about Jesus as a condemned man who struggled with a violent death that he did not deserve, as well as a separation from his Father so complete some call it hell. His anguish was so stark that he sweat drops of blood.

This scene makes the Christmas story of the baby in the manger even more profound. The second scene in these verses from Luke shows Jesus finding the disciples asleep. Jesus' warning to them is still relevant in 2020, *"Get up and pray that you may not come into the time of trial."* Like Jesus, all Christians still struggle with evil in this world.

Lord, help me focus on you and not all of the other distractions this time of year. Enlighten me so that I will not be spiritually or emotionally asleep this holiday season. Draw me to you as I pray that I "may not come into the time of trial."

TUESDAY, DECEMBER 15

Read Isaiah 9:1-7.

"For a child has been born for us, a son given to us; authority rests upon his shoulders; and he is named Wonderful Counselor, Mighty God, Everlasting Father, Prince of Peace. His authority shall grow continually, and there shall be endless peace for the throne of David and his kingdom. He will establish and uphold it with justice and with righteousness from this time onward and forevermore. The zeal of the LORD of hosts will do this ."— Isaiah 9:6-7

MANY KNOW that the prophet Isaiah lived around 700 years before Jesus was born. The striking thing to me here is not only the accuracy of the prophecy but the knowledge that our God loves me so much. He knew that I would miss the mark and desperately need a Savior. Thus, the Lord was not surprised at my plight and made a plan to save me hundreds of years (at least) before Jesus was born in a manger.

When times are difficult or discouraging, it is such an encouragement to know that even when I am blindsided, God is not surprised. He always understands what I need whether it be the energy to battle the Christmas shopping rush or the reminder in times of family stress that my worth is in him only. I am precious because I am made in God's image and redeemed by his blood.

Lord, help me to remain confident that, even in this busy season, your love for me truly is a "Love Divine, All Loves Excelling."

WEDNESDAY, DECEMBER 16

Read Mark 1:1-8.

"The beginning of the good news of Jesus Christ, the Son of God. As it is written in the prophet Isaiah, 'See, I am sending my messenger ahead of you, who will prepare your way; the voice of one crying out in the wilderness: "Prepare the way of the Lord, make his paths straight,"' John the baptizer appeared in the wilderness, proclaiming a baptism of repentance for the forgiveness of sins. And people from the whole Judean countryside and all the people of Jerusalem were going out to him, and were baptized by him in the river Jordan, confessing their sins ."— Mark 1:1-5

IN THIS GOSPEL STORY, God sends out a messenger to prepare for the coming of Christ. I think this idea of preparing cuts even more deeply now when we are in a season of preparation. In the church, we light the Advent wreath, wear blue, and sing songs like, "O Come, O Come Emmanuel." In the world, we see Santa Claus on every commercial, run from store to store, and worry about who will show up for Christmas dinner.

Two things strike me when I read this passage. First, John the Baptist was a little bit of an odd bird. He appears in the wilderness to preach, not on the street corner where most people will hear him. In the next verse, we are told that John wore a vest of camel hair and ate locusts.

John was unconventional even at his time in history. At the local high school, John would definitely not have been invited to the popular kids' table. But Scripture reminds us, *"The Lord does not see as mortals see; they look on the outward appearance, but the Lord looks on the heart."* (1 Samuel 16:7).

Secondly, God sent a messenger out ahead of his Son, and the people responded. Does God still send us out? Most of us would agree that he does, but we don't want to have to go out in the backwoods (however that looks to us). We don't want to be the oddball that stands out, or the person others (even in the church) don't get.

Help us, Lord, not to be afraid of appearances this Advent and Christmas season and to open our hearts to you.

THURSDAY, DECEMBER 17

Read 2 Peter 2:10-16.
"These people, however, are like irrational animals, mere creatures of instinct, born to be caught and killed. They slander what they do not understand, and when those creatures are destroyed, they also will be destroyed, suffering the penalty for doing wrong." — 2 Peter 2:12-13a

HERE PETER REFERS to people who slander and destroy others as "animals." I can't help but think these verses could apply to the sin of racism that still plagues our country. Martin Luther King, Jr. echoed these Scriptures: "Like an unchecked cancer, hate corrodes the personality and eats away its vital unity. Hate destroys a man's sense of values and his objectivity."

I think God weeps when we put on "our uniforms" and judge and dismiss others who are on a different "team."

I had the opportunity a few years ago to take a college class I was teaching to meet with a Justice Department official who worked during the Kennedy presidency. John Siegenthaler knew Dr. King during the 1960s and was telling us firsthand stories about him. When one student asked him what one word he would use to describe MLK, he answered, "Love."

Lord, help us to remember all human beings are precious and valuable because you created them in your image. You loved all of us so much that Jesus redeemed us by his blood. And in the words of Dr. King himself, help us decide to "stick with love. Hate is too great a burden to bear."

FRIDAY, DECEMBER 18

Read Matthew 11:2-15.

*"When John heard in prison what the Messiah was doing, he
sent word by his disciples and said to him, 'Are you the one
who is to come, or are we to wait for another?' Jesus answered
them, 'Go and tell John what you hear and see: the blind
receive their sight, the lame walk, the lepers are cleansed, the
deaf hear, the dead are raised, and the poor have good news
brought to them. And blessed is anyone who takes no offense
at me.'" —Matthew 11:2-6*

HERE WE HAVE ANOTHER Advent reading about
John the Baptist. He was in prison but wanted to know
who Jesus really was. In fact, he's betting his very life on
the answer. Jesus doesn't directly answer with a simple yes
or no. Instead, he talks about the miracles the disciples
have seen: sight for the blind, paralytics walking, lepers
cleansed, hearing for the deaf, dead resurrected, and good
news for the poor. If Jesus was applying for a job, there
would be no need to beef up his resume.

Some say that Jesus was speaking only metaphorically
here. He was really saying we are all spiritually dead, blind,
deaf, unclean, and need to be healed. And, of course, that
is true. But it also seems that Jesus had an uncanny knack
of knowing a person's top card—the nagging issue that
drove them to him. And just as in a game, the top card

has to be played before the lower cards can be dealt with. In a world filled with controversial politics, hate speech, neglect of the suffering among us, and materialism gone wild, I often don't even know my one real need. What a comfort it is that God loves me, he knows me, and he sent his Son as the Messiah to help and save me.

Thank you, Lord, for meeting me at the point of my need.

SATURDAY, DECEMBER 19

Read Jude 1:19-25.

"Now to him who is able to keep you from falling, and to make you stand without blemish in the presence of his glory with rejoicing, to the only God our Savior, through Jesus Christ our Lord, be glory, majesty, power, and authority, before all time and now and forever. Amen." — *Jude 1:24-25*

JUDE IS NOT a book in the New Testament that I think of much. But as we enter into the fourth Sunday of Advent, it might be good to consider it. These two verses remind us that we are not able to save ourselves from falling into sin and the law. It doesn't matter if I don't get to all of the Christmas activities. It doesn't matter if I buy the perfect presents. It doesn't matter what my church members or even my family think of me. The Savior presents us, *"without blemish in the presence of his glory."* And Jude tells us that we will be "rejoicing" when we see God face to face. What a promise! What a comfort!

Jesus, help remind me daily that heaven is my true home.

Our King and Savior now draws near: Come, let us adore him.

Book of Common Prayer, Morning
Prayer II, Advent Antiphon

JOY

Fourth Sunday of Advent

Purify our conscience, Almighty God, by your daily visitation, that your Son Jesus Christ, at his coming, may find; who lives and reigns with you, in the unity of the Holy Spirit, one God, now and for ever. *Amen.*

Book of Common Prayer, Collect for the Fourth Sunday of Advent

Sunday, December 20

Read Luke 1:46-55.
"And Mary said, 'My soul magnifies the Lord, and my spirit rejoices in God my Savior, for he has looked with favor on the lowliness of his servant. Surely, from now on all generations will call me blessed." — Luke 1:46-48

BLESSED. Mary pours her heart out praising the greatness of God for choosing a lowly servant to be the vessel that births the promised gift of God. Joyfully and gratefully praising God, Mary's obedience is a heart song, exalting and giving all credit to God. Blessed equates to humble servitude and favor with God.

Word meanings certainly morph over time. Facebook, Instagram, and Twitter postings of #blessed display pictures or statements of satisfaction from vacations, homes, cars, friends, entertainment, and food. #Blessed typically depicts personal satisfaction of "living the best life"—a life of privilege and comfort.

What blessed "song" does your life project? Blessed as a servant of God? Or blessed fulfillment from earthly pleasures?

Jesus, show us a glimpse of Mary's soul so we too may rejoice in the blessing of serving you.

Monday, December 21

Read Isaiah 11:1-9.

"A shoot shall come out from the stump of Jesse, and a branch shall grow out of his roots." — Isaiah 11:1

"WHO ARE YOUR PEOPLE?" After initially greeting a new acquaintance, my dad always asked the question, "Who are your people?" The inquiry was like a pruning exercise, watching a master gardener digging to find the taproot, the root that anchors. The discovery would shine light on family lineage, characteristics, beliefs, purpose, and connection. Roots matter!

Jesse's youngest son, David, was anointed by the prophet Samuel for future kingship. At baptism, we also are anointed and sealed as Christ's own forever grafting us into the family of God and rooting us for eternity. Roots matter!

Lord, create in our hearts and souls a longing for connection, to dig deep, to find our grafting in the roots of Jesus.

Tuesday, December 22

Read Hebrews 10:35-11:1.

"Now faith is the assurance of things hoped for, the conviction of things not seen."— Hebrews 11:1

ADVENT CALENDARS HUNG on the kitchen walls as children scampered to open the December 22nd door, revealing the message inside. Someone felt the anticipation that 25 days in December brought to children, young and old. The feeling sparked in the 1850s led to the Advent daily calendar activity with doors numbered 1 through 25. Each day another open door revealed a Scripture portion of the Nativity story. The object of the calendar was to focus hearts on Christ and his coming as the Savior of the world. Advent refers to the first coming of Christ to earth. *"The Word became flesh and lived among us, and we have seen his glory, the glory as of a father's only son, full of grace and truth"* (John 1:14).

Yet, that is not the only Advent. There will be a second Advent when Jesus comes again. Let us follow the example of children as we live in faith certain of what we hope for and certain of what we do not see.

Lord, may our focused anticipation of your second Advent bring daily excitement filled with the certainty of seeing the Savior.

WEDNESDAY, DECEMBER 23

Read Luke 1:26-38.

"'You will conceive in your womb and bear a son, and you will name him Jesus.'... The angel said to her, 'The Holy Spirit will come upon you, and the power of the Most High will overshadow you; therefore the child to be born will be holy; he will be called Son of God.'"— Luke 1:31-35

THE ANGEL APPEARED to Mary telling her she would bear a child and the things her Son would accomplish. When she answered, *"let it be with me according to your word"* (1:38b), I wonder if she could truly comprehend to what it was that she was assenting. Mark Lowry wrote a poignant song called "Mary, Did You Know?" that speaks to the heart of Mary:

> "Did you know that your baby boy has come to make you new? This child that you've delivered, will soon deliver you... Did you know that your baby boy has walked where angels trod? When you kiss your little baby, you kiss the face of God... Did you know that your baby boy is heaven's perfect lamb? That sleeping child you're holding is the great I AM. Mary did you know?"

This fourth Sunday of Advent is often filled with pageants recalling Mary and Joseph's journey to Bethlehem and the birth of Jesus. As hearts and minds grasp the image of a beautiful bouncing baby boy placed in Mary's arms, may we realize she's holding the Great I AM. The Son of God came in humble human fashion to make things new and deliver us.

Lord, today we stand in awe that a young girl submitted in total obedience to the message of your angel.

Thursday, December 24

Read Philippians 2:5-11.
"Therefore God also highly exalted him and gave him the name that is above every name, so that at the name of Jesus every knee should bend, in heaven and on earth and under the earth, and every tongue should confess that Jesus Christ is Lord, to the glory of God the Father." — Philippians 2:9-11

PAUL ENCOURAGES US to be Christ-minded, demonstrating his love and acceptance of one another. We are to humble ourselves laying aside differences and self-ambition for the good of all. Jesus willingly sacrificed becoming obedient to death. And, God elevated him above all so every knee would bow at the mention of his name.

On this eve of great anticipation and preparation for the one that has come and the yet to come again, let our tongues confess that Jesus Christ is the Lord of our lives. May we strive to be like-minded with Christ, and let our knees hit the ground at the sound of his name, Jesus.

Lord, let us sing like the angels, "Glory to God in the highest heaven, and on earth peace among those whom he favors!" (Luke 2:14). Gloria in excelsis Deo!

CHRISTMAS DAY, DECEMBER 25

Read Titus 2:11-14.

"For the grace of God has appeared, bringing salvation to all, training us to renounce impiety and worldly passions, and in the present age to live lives that are self-controlled, upright, and godly, while we wait for the blessed hope and the manifestation of the glory of our great God and Savior, Jesus Christ. He it is who gave himself for us that he might redeem us from all iniquity and purify for himself a people of his own who are zealous for good deeds."— Titus 2:11-14

THE 2020 #1 BEST GIFT! Here is the gift that solves the worldly issues, creates equality of all people, restores hope, and humbles us in reverence to Jesus. The gift Jesus hands us is salvation.

Remembering the past is important. Hindsight offers wisdom and clarity. The hope that once lay in a manger is now manifest in the saving acts of one man, Jesus Christ.

Lord, let us put aside all worldly passions and be zealous for good deeds resting assured in you as we anticipate your coming again.

SMALL GROUP
STUDY GUIDE

HOPE

Getting Started

- What special gift do you most remember hoping you would receive for Christmas? Share that memory.

- Watch the video for this week. Find the videos for small group discussion at biblestudymedia.com/advent2020.

- Read Psalm 80:1-7.

Questions for Discussion

1. The psalm's author refers to God right at the start as, "Shepherd of Israel." How does this image speak to the need for help?

2. The psalmist expressed a deep longing for restoration from God. What do you think the prayer "let your face shine" means?

3. What does salvation look like for those who hope in the Lord?

4. There are several petitions in these verses. What do they teach you about prayer?

5. The psalmist is sure that the Lord is Israel's only defense or hope. Do you regard the Lord as your only hope? If so, does your life reflect that?

6. How would seeing the light of God's face change the circumstances in your life? Does this give you an eternal hope?

_____

_____

_____

_____

_____

_____

_____

_____

_____

_____

PEACE

Getting Started

- *Close your eyes and envision an easel with a canvas before you with the word "Peace" in the center. On the canvas is a picture of peace comprised of words. What words would draw your picture of peace? For example, contentment, security.*

- *Watch the video for this week. Find the videos for small group discussion at biblestudymedia.com/advent2020.*

- *Read Psalm 85:8-13.*

Questions for Discussion

1. What do you think it means to be righteous? How is faithfulness described in the psalm (vs. 8-9)?

2. What do you think it means when it says in verse 10, "Steadfast love and faithfulness will meet; righteousness and peace will kiss each other"?

3. What benefits does God offer those who turn their hearts to God in this Psalm (vs. 12-13)?

4. The psalm points to the way of relationship with God. How are we made right with God?

5. How does faithfulness sustain our spiritual lives like the crops that spring up from the ground?

6. Verse 12 speaks of increased yield. How do you know God has given you this increase? If God offers us peace through faithfulness and righteousness, how can you know the peace that surpasses understanding?

_____

_____

_____

_____

_____

_____

_____

_____

_____

_____

_____

_____

_____

LOVE

Getting Started

- In the 1970s movie, "Love Story", there was a famous line, "Love means never having to say you're sorry." If you could define love with a word or simple phrase, what would you say?

- Watch the video for this week. Find the videos for small group discussion at biblestudymedia.com/advent2020.

- Read Isaiah 61:1-11.

Questions for Discussion

1. Compare this beginning of this reading to Luke 4:16-21. Who is the speaker? Why is that important?

2. In verses 10-11, the bridegroom and the bride are the symbols. What is the significance of these symbols?

3. How does the Lord make many righteous?

4. In verses 2-3, the Scriptures describe how God will care for those who mourn. Does this picture give you hope in grief?

5. Verse 7 gives an impression of what our inheritance
   from our Father will be. What does this say to you about
   God's love for you?

6. In what ways do you "greatly rejoice in the Lord"
   (vs. 10)? How might you encourage that joy in God's
   love for you?

_____

_____

_____

_____

_____

_____

_____

_____

_____

_____

_____

_____

_____

Joy

Getting Started

- *What is the one thing that's brought you the most joy in your life?*

- *Watch the video for this week. Find the videos for small group discussion at biblestudymedia.com/advent2020.*

- *Read Luke 1:46-55.*

Questions for Discussion

1. *What do you think it means when Mary says, "My soul magnifies the Lord"?*

2. *Where do you hear or find Mary's joy in this Scripture? What are the sources of Mary's joy?*

3. *How are Mary's hopes and dreams for herself and her people expressed in her prayer of rejoicing?*

4. *Do you have an awareness of God's unique plan for your life? How would awareness of that purpose bring you joy?*

5. *Mary was chosen to be the God-bearer (Greek: Theotokos). How are we called to be God-bearers in the world?*

6. *How can we share the joy of being a child of God with others?*

_____

_____

_____

_____

_____

_____

_____

_____

_____

_____

_____

_____

_____

_____

_____

_____

_____

MARCIA HOTCHKISS has been married to the Rev. Thomas Hotchkiss for 34 years, including two years as a seminary spouse and 26 years as the wife of an ordained clergy person. During that time, they have moved seven times as Tom has served in eight different churches. Marcia has taught Christian formation classes at the various churches as well as led Bible studies and spoken at retreats. Marcia has taught communications at various colleges, including interpersonal dynamics, group communication, and public speaking. She has a certificate in spiritual direction from a three-year ecumenical program. Marcia has also been trained as a circle of trust facilitator by a protégé of Parker Palmer.

She is the co-author of a public speaking textbook as well as "View from the Pew," a clergy spouse Bible study. Marcia has also written for The Living Church and The Anglican Digest. Together with her husband, Marcia writes a blog www.midlifecontemplative.com. The couple is also the designers and facilitators of a marriage retreat aimed particularly for clergy people and their spouses. Marcia is the event's chair of Spiritual Ministries Institute in the DFW area which promotes contemplative practices.

Marcia and Tom have two grown sons and a one-year-old granddaughter, who is the light of their lives. She enjoys reading, movies, traveling, and pickleball.

GILDA HURST has called McKinney, TX home for almost a decade. She is a licensed career educator who spent over twenty years as a classroom teacher, developed programs for school districts, served as a crisis professional and teacher mentor. She has ministered in church communities in Tennessee, Kentucky, and Texas to youth and adults.

She is an evangelist at heart living out the example of Christ wherever she goes. Gilda was received into The Order of Evangelism in the Episcopal Diocese of Dallas in 2019. She has been married to The Rev. Michael Hurst for 39 years. Together they have led marriage enrichment retreats, taught Christian education, and hosted incredible parish social gatherings. However, her favorite pasttime is spending adventurous days with her five grandchildren.

Gilda holds a degree in Vocational Careers with Children and Human Development from Western Kentucky University, and she did post-graduate religion studies at The School of Theology at The University of the South and The Stanton Center for Ministry Formation. She is a licensed spiritual director and the co-author of "View from the Pew," a clergy spouse Bible study.

Bible Study Media

Bible Study Media believes in building up the Church through a fresh discovery of God's Word and Spirit.

We produce resources to shape hearts and minds around the patterns of Christ while strengthening community. Our Bible studies invite participants to journey together through the Scriptures in the rhythms of the Christian year.

We want to support churches! Our devotions and bible studies are timed to complement the Revised Common Lectionary (a common Scripture reading plan) which appoints the lessons for worship services for over half the Christian churches around the world.

We invite you to explore Bible Study Media's Ignite community—**Igniting Hearts and Engaging Minds.**

members.biblestudymedia.com

THE CRUCIFIED LIFE: SEVEN WORDS FROM THE CROSS

Discover what it means to pick up your cross and follow Jesus.

The Crucified Life small group Christian study is designed to reflect upon the Seven Last Words of Christ from the cross and what they mean for us today.

Walk the road of Calvary with Jesus in order to grow closer to Him. The Crucified Life small group study examines human suffering as it is mirrored in Christ's suffering on the cross and what His seven last words say to a hurting world. Find out incredible insights into these words as Jesus teaches us, even in death, how we can use our suffering and triumph over it for His glory.

biblestudymedia.com/the-crucified-life

CPSIA information can be obtained
at www.ICGtesting.com
Printed in the USA
JSHW040950031120
9264JS00002B/8

9 781942 243410